Emu, Gecko and the Little Boy

Retold by Alex Barlow
Illustrated by Elizabeth Djandilnga Thorne

M

A little boy was lost in the bush. He had gone out with his parents whilst they hunted and looked for food. Gradually the little boy was left behind as his parents went further and further into the bush.

From time to time he would call out, "Mother! Father! Hey!", to let them know he was safe. An emu who was also looking for food nearby heard the boy as he kept calling out. She looked around and, as there was no sign of any other people, she decided to steal the boy. She listened when the boy called out to hear if anyone answered. No one answered, so Emu called back to the boy, "Hey!"

The boy had a light spear made of cane. He was looking for fruit on the bushes. He would look carefully for ripe fruit. When he saw some wild gooseberries he would throw his spear into the bush and try to knock them down.

Emu led the boy deeper into the bush. Each time he called out, "Mother! Father! Hey!" Emu would call back, "Hey!" The little boy followed her call. He thought it was his mother and father calling back to him. Every now and then he stopped to throw his spear into a bush to knock down more fruit. He was quite happy. He had plenty of fruit to eat and the tart juice of the wild gooseberries stopped him from getting thirsty. He thought his parents were nearby and that they would soon find him when they were ready to return to their camp.

It was late afternoon. By now Emu had led the boy so far into the bush away from his parents and their camp that they would never be able to find him. Emu hid herself in a large bush and called out, "Hey!" The little boy was growing tired. He thought it was about time his parents took him home.

Emu called out again, "Hey!" The sound came from a large, thick bush up ahead. The little boy started to walk towards the bush. "Hey!" called Emu. The call sounded closer so the little boy hurried on to the bush. He looked on one side of it but he couldn't see anyone. Emu was crouching down in the middle of the bush. The little boy looked all around the bush. He called out, "Mother! Father! Hey!" This time no one answered. Emu stayed crouched down hiding in the bush. The little boy began to grow frightened. He could not see his mother and father anywhere. "Father! Mother! Hey!" he called.

Then Emu jumped out of the bush and grabbed him. The boy screamed with fright. Emu tried to quieten him. "It's only me here," she said, "only me. I'll look after you. I'll be your mother now. Look, it's only me. You can be my son."

She lifted the little boy up and put him on her back. She carried him along to her camp. On the way she stopped at a pool to catch tadpoles to take back for food.

Gecko, her husband, was waiting for her back in camp.

"I found this little boy lost in the bush," she told Gecko. "His parents went off and left him. I found him so now he is mine. He is my son. I will be a mother to him."

"No," said Gecko. "He is not your son. You stole him from them. You are telling lies. Where did you steal him from? He is not your son, he is still theirs."

"He's mine," said Emu. "I found him. His parents just left him. They didn't want him. I found him so he's my son now."

"You stole him," said Gecko. "You must send him back to his people."

"I'm going to keep him," Emu said. "They didn't want him. I found him. They left him for me."

Gecko was very angry with Emu and he argued with her for a long time. Emu would not agree to send the boy back to his parents. Finally, they all laid down to sleep.

Just before dawn the next day, Emu went off to get more food.

14

Gecko had been thinking all night what was the best thing to do. He knew Emu would not give up the boy. He could not take the boy back to his parents. If he did, Emu would be angry. The boy's parents might be angry with Emu, too. They might follow Gecko's tracks back to their camp. They might kill Emu.

Emu went looking for more tadpoles. She gathered hundreds of them and cooked them. She divided the cooked tadpoles into separate heaps for herself, for Gecko and for the boy.

As soon as Emu left the camp, Gecko went into the bush and gathered bark fibre to make a rope. Back in camp he began to roll the bark on his thigh. He kept on rolling the bark and making the rope until late afternoon. Then he took the rope he had made and buried it in the sand. He gathered up the pieces of bark fibre left over and scattered them in the bush.

When Emu arrived home with the cooked parcels of tadpoles they all sat and ate the food she had brought. Once more they laid down to sleep.

Before dawn Emu was up and off gathering tadpoles to cook. Gecko worked all day on his rope, hiding it away and clearing up the leftover pieces before Emu came home with their supper.

Many days passed like this. Gecko's plan was to make a very long rope. From time to time he would tell the boy to take one end of the rope and to walk with it until he ran out of rope. When he reached the end of the rope the boy would give it a tug to let Gecko know. One day the boy said that he had reached almost halfway back to his parents' camp.

At last Gecko thought the rope was long enough. "Tie it around you," he told the boy. "When you reach your parents' camp give the rope a good shake. Do it three times so that I know you are there. Then untie the rope and go to your people."

The little boy did as Gecko had told him. As soon as he saw his parents' camp he shook the rope three times and stepped out of it. His parents looked up and saw him coming. His mother's sisters were all there in the camp with her. They thought the little boy might be dead. They were there to mourn with his mother. "Oh, my goodness," his mother cried when she saw him. "Here he is!"

In the late afternoon back at the camp Gecko lay resting. When Emu arrived she looked around for the little boy to give him his supper. She could not see him anywhere. She put down the parcels of food and went to look for him. "I can't see him anywhere," she said to Gecko.
"He should be there. He might be playing around. I haven't seen him. I've been resting," said Gecko.

Emu searched everywhere. She couldn't find him. At last, as it was growing dark, she found his tracks. She followed them for a little way. When it was too dark to see any more she left a marker so that she could start to follow the little boy as soon as it was light. She did not suspect that Gecko had helped the little boy because she saw only the boy's tracks.

Next day she ran following the boy's tracks. He had walked a long way passing many places on his way back to his parents' camp. Emu ran past these places till finally she came to their camp. The people had had a feast of turtle and dugong to welcome back the boy. Pieces of turtle and dugong were hanging in a tree to dry. A stringy bark canoe was hauled up on the bank near their camp.

"Where is the boy?" Emu said to them. "I want him. You bring him out to me straightaway."

The boy's family were afraid that Emu would come looking for him. They had thought of a way that they might trick her. They had put armbands on the boy's arms, feathers around his waist and necklaces on his neck. Then they wrapped him in sheets of paperbark as they do a dead child. Emu demanded that they give her the little boy. They pointed to the body wrapped in paperbark.

"Unwrap him. Show me him," she said. "Bring him out to show me or I'll pull the sky down on you."

The people were too frightened to say no. They unwrapped the boy and stood him in front of Emu.

26

"Hey, little fellow, you belong to me," said Emu, kissing and hugging the little boy. She made his people give her dugong and other presents and away she went with the little boy back to her own camp.

When Emu arrived back at their camp with the boy, the dugong and all the presents she had made the people give her, Gecko was very angry.

"You are a thief," he told her. "Now you really have stolen this boy from his family. You have no excuse. You are just greedy. That's it. I'm finished with you. From now on I'll stay by myself."

As Gecko went around the camp gathering up all his things, Emu pleaded with him to stay. She kept on arguing that she did not steal the boy, that she had found him in the first place by chance.

"You are a thief now," Gecko said angrily. "I'm finished with you." He threw a handful of burning coals from the fire at her. He left her and went up into the sky to become thunder and lightning.

Sadly, Emu watched him go. She didn't want the little boy any more. She sent him back to his parents' camp. To this day Emu wanders sadly through the wattle scrub.

In this story it was the little boy's fault for not keeping up with his parents. He had already wandered out of touch with them before Emu saw him. Although he called to his parents, he did not listen for their call. He was naughty and his capture by Emu was his punishment. Emu, in turn, is punished for being a thief and a liar.